Passenger

Also by Tom Thompson

Live Feed
The Pitch

Passenger

Tom Thompson

Four Way Books
Tribeca

Library of Congress Cataloging-in-Publication Data

Names: Thompson, Tom, 1967- author.
Title: Passenger / Tom Thompson.
Description: New York, NY : Four Way Books, [2018]
Identifiers: LCCN 2018003718 | ISBN 9781945588235 (pbk. : alk. paper)
Classification: LCC PS3620.H69 A6 2018 | DDC 811/.6--dc23
LC record available at https://lccn.loc.gov/2018003718

This book is manufactured in the United States of America and printed on acid-free paper.

Four Way Books is a not-for-profit literary press. We are grateful for the assistance
we receive from individual donors, public arts agencies, and private foundations.

This publication is made possible with public funds from the New York State Council on the Arts, a
state agency.

PROUD MEMBER

We are a proud member of the Community of Literary Magazines and Presses.

For M.

For W.

For F.

A kelson of the creation is love.

Contents

Did I grow or did I stay?
Did I vanish or decay?

1. Homage to the EEG

The Body and the Bed

First there were whispers.
Then a fizzing
behind the eyes,

a tongue of light,
a fit of flame,
a spidering sound like rain

smattering a tarp
or a lit cigarette
doused in a sink.

There was a pointed series
of breaths and shaking
disquiet. I was possessed.

No. Shot through
with garnet like molasses,
like meat.

I could not wish to be rid of it.
Rubber socks and quarter-inch bands
dictated blood flow

until I became a pillar of hellfire
torqued about
by a gown of love.

I was waking and static
and swaddled in sweat.
Adoration

was my trainer or I
was its flunky, either way
there was work to be done

and I was the one
having it done to me.

Interictal

There's the smell of burnt wires
when you come to, and eggy sweat.
Episcopalian canticles

rise up the air shaft with fish tacos.
Small dogs press their lips
to living room glass. Light

shivers like a cell.
Some call this a disturbance of the animal
functions of the soul.

You know it as fatigue,
how time sometimes
gets out in front of you.

Once, they'd have shouted
Holy Holy at your head
or drowned you for a witch.

It's hard to breathe.
Ethereal prick, you'd call out
if your mouth could move.

Your material substance rings
with what you can't say.
Earth floats

in the window pane, pendulous
fruit that's consumed its tree.
Is it too much oxygen

streaming through your helmet
or is it just you,
riding empty swells

for five or fifteen seconds, until
the bell
of everything else

goes under-the-sea green?

Surgeon

You're patient, but
rattled, vertical
in swimming-pool blue.

The body under your thumb
is rim to rim
one shallow piece of skin,

an alien,
quivering tambourine
you slip your hand in.

Out in the oxygen courtyard
we drift, dull as bees.
The air between us

is an open, boisterous sea.
A chime
could cross it, as a chasm

fills with the ring
of a climber's
shiny dropped instrument.

An Orderly

One white figure
stands at the screen, gathers
others.

They cluster
around your machine
as gulls

cluster and gather
at a cliff.
Who says you exist?

Ice stumbles, falls
in the ice box
down the hall.

Locks rattle
visiting room doors.
Don't move,

not even for flies,
those precise delegates
that will not let your blood be.

"Strike that." "So what."
"Fuck you." "For drinks."
Light draws the eye

to boxes
piled on boxes, little
refineries of memory

that blink on and off, analyzing
protein counts
in lemon and lime,

articulating human matter
as chemical shift,
as pure information.

Without story, without a single
communicable word,
the room's adamantine architecture

is openly violated
by laughter.
Whose violation? Whose

rigorous prototype? On what
planet bathed
in bacterial light?

Breath on the Mirror

Of course there is another world. But it is not elsewhere.
—Max Ritvo

We believe that time has no color, no odor,
and that respiration occurs without color or odor.

Still, we observe the event
as a luster on skin, a familiar off-plum scent.

The infection grows rampant, feeds on itself
in this compromised respiratory tract.

It takes the name "our nature" and makes arrangements.
Together, we record the dilation of pupils,

register the alteration of oral bacterial flora.
The agent needs oxygen if it's to breathe as we do.

We're coating our mirrors with glue.

Ode to the Electrodes Fixed to Your Scalp

Neural clusters swim in place
        as grass in wind or galaxies
  self-pulsing. Electro-

encephalograph night
        composed of green light.
  It clicks

like rain on a metal roof,
        clicks
  and clicks on shadow,

ignites shadow, close shadow,
        so-close-it's-a-rude-
  bloom-in-your-face shadow.

The machine that governs your lungs
        darts breath in only for you
  to push it out again.

The breath of us forms
        a moth-white crown around
  your head, evaporates.

Your pupils are over-large,
      a torrential dark
    anyone breathing could drown in.

Here, further in,
      a fine speck, a pistil
    shining in fog. "What you love

you become," said Clare
      in self-hacked hair and wool.

Turning as a Kind of Shouting

Total night or absolute
          morning, either way the bed
    was a ragged, tumbling thing.

You were only trying to
          keep still in it.
    Cicadas nuzzled each

other in the trench out back.
          This is what you said
    you wanted, it was

"dead quiet," and yet
          the window rattled its tracks,
    rattled birds who mistook it

for air. There was a smudge
          on the glass you took
    for ghost, a dream

you couldn't shake
          enough to exit. Chugging trucks
    slammed doors shut,

idling opalescent exhaust—
        breathed out, breathed out—
a mineral cloud

that stirred a fern in your lungs,
        cracked open your eyes
to a speckled dark

where you woke, humid,
        as it is
inside the hold of a ship.

Stout Cortez

It is a conqueror's light. I'm sure I've seen a conqueror's light in the eyes of
these ancient children perched on the cliff of the new world,

the ones for whom the order "to survey" comes in the same urgent
whispers as the instruction to fail and fall.

The edge of the cliff extends endlessly over the infinite valley. Would
such slender bodies smash to the ground if they fell or simply float there,
forever?

Without a sense of the language of the place, without hope of trade, the
route back congeals like a scrape in skin.

It's like you can't keep anything inside your body anymore, not protein-
rich bugs, not suicide fruit, not the bark of a tree, not your sketchiest
prospects, not even fate.

See how the moon retches up even its most sober tea?

Hurry up. Return to your life. The lightning you see by in bursts threatens
the ships that brought you.

If you spot a conqueror limping, he's still got his weapon. Keep on.

If you spy a conqueror asleep in the crown of a tree, he's simply striving to follow the sun. Keep on. Keep on.

Magic evolves here into something swifter, more "in time." Progress? That's another matter.

Stout Cortez, you summon the world with your violent melancholy and your arms comply like two exhausted armies.

It is the music, the striking idiot music, of *Let fly*.

Death Is Death

All my Christians on Vimeo, smashing
their tambourines, trying to make it
through the Book of Revelations like a tiny

hurricane makes it through a stifling
afternoon, trying to whip through a morbid
endless loop and die just one more time.

At Teen Jesus, we talked for hours
after the five-hundred-mile trip, each of us
frantic with road exhaust in his separate

teeny hollow—wondering, accusing, faltering,
How will I be saved? I pressed the question
into the palms of the next day

when the shuddering sail strapped
to my shoulders and crotch rose me up
and higher up, struck me wooden

with panic—as all the pretty
counselors beamed and waved.
All my Christians now, decades on,

trying to take the whole thing private.
They've wheeled the founder out to reach
and rally us across our flickering devices . . .

To hell with your money, Savior.
To hell with your little stone door
that leads out and out but never in.

The Door that Leads In and In but Never Out

There's a boy who stands where the door should be.
He seems so certain, posing with his secrets intact,
pulling us forward by what we cannot say.

Do we trust him? There's no mark of God or country
on him, no signs of madness in the width
and whiteness of his eyes. But the hair self-yanked

into its angular, public shape betrays him
as one who has nothing to do with the body
he's standing in. How would a doctor classify

this work of not knowing, that it's impossible
or temporary or just in our heads?
What would anyone who can speak say

to those who were born in the trees,
who can detect a squall in the open distant sea,
open as it is to you, to me.

The Very Image of a Child

Sweet sweet sweet sweet sweet
    as crème caramel in a cup,
as a May flower calling a swarm of ants
    to tear open its tight green dress.

You lie on your face
    putting your tongue to plump yellow
dandelion pie. You smash burnt-sugar
    windows and lick up the shards.

Your hunger terrifies me.
    It roils the ocean in a cove
they call the Devil's Asshole.
    And yet your ravenous power

is composed of tenderness!
    A furious delicacy known also to spiders
who've gone all fat and juicy and spin
    through acres of dead space.

We both want what the spider does,
    endless possible children,
even as it detonates
    egg sac after egg into the wind.

Filaments extend
    across parkways and barbed wire,
door cracks and downspouts,
    as the spinneret swells with the sap

of corpse after corpse. A strand or two
    will surely catch in the trees
as bleached traces of tinsel, will stray
    around the wrists and not decay.

What could any professional say,
    having seen how some storms pass
such a long, long way through
    a single skull, and some storms stay.

Peak Phosphorous

A phosphorescent apogee is simply a phosphorescent apogee.
You can't transcend it with sulfur or lawyers or psychotropic medicine.

There are certain delicate individuals who possess it from birth.
They're prone to daydream, to wander off,

are susceptible to glistening wounds and crippling headaches.
Certain devices pick up traces here and there in the cerebral cortex.

This small metal box, for one, extrudes a tangle of wires
secured on the other end to your scalp.

It records light-based data you might feel as a vacancy
fizzing up out of yourself

as a plant froths in high summer, or a nebula swells up
to swallow itself whole, making the next nuclear event.

You wanted to see where it all goes when the stop comes,
that moment you're nowhere recorded as absolute departure.

Homage to Alcohol

Did you forget something? Maybe
back in Wiesbaden or Cologne?
Tears seem so clear from this distance,

a sugar memory at work
in see through cells. Like sheep's wool
in summer, your capacity for tumult

makes anyone who touches you sweat.
It's all bloomy-hot: floorboards
grown soft, ribs bled on a paper plate

with ragged sailor on the side,
paint chips flopped big as lettuce leaves
off the walls, antique flowers

puffed up, brazen with rust.
You don't know anything
about this place, do you?

That's why you keep turning back
to me. Bodies pass within centimeters
of your hips. Humidity beads

on the skin where you wait, all ear.
How many years have you
consumed yourself? Swallowing

creatures who swallow you,
so thick with breath you can't breathe.
You don't want anyone's

dissolution, it's just what happens.
Like the air in this club that smells
so much of rot. Like a boy's

face emerging from the stall,
caught
neck-deep in rising thoughts.

Ictus

Do you conclude that this is all,
that this succession of half-

struck states leads to catastrophe
both lasting and true?

Called *absence*, an opposite
ghost I can reach and hold onto

but is still not present.
Together, let's render

homage to the set of electrical
conditions that speaks

a squall in brain salts
and stops a body cold.

Disease or gift, let's render it.
As to Caesar?

As to a butcher
to whom each calf is delivered

with a hidden name,
a name kept secret from every handler,

that the rancher keeps secret especially
from himself.

Progression

The stillness that takes this child
is a gold lagoon.

On the surface you can see the trees
and the clouds circling.

The lagoon thickens.
It doesn't see, it consumes.

You and I together
compose the eye.

We come to say "storm in the brain"
when what we have has no name.

( )

Visitor

When the dead come knocking,
the road goes clear, elastic
as duodenum. You can see forever,

the area blasted free of its citizens.
All that's left is feeling, silk purse hairs
kissing your dead prick

and the ghosts all hands—
which is why when you cry out
you cry so quietly.

No one can hear you but the ethereal
road. It's just the road. It's just the road
shushing you toward the sea,

the salt mess of it cooked
to a sensate pitch. The road understands
nothing of the pelvic bone

(which is your secret). The bone
knows nothing of the combustion it frames
(which is your secret). Your electro-chemical

switch is so innocent! To say nothing
of the collapsible mass
it's bent around. It's bent around you.

Debridement

The spirit is weakest at the outer layers.
But there are cells, or "chimes,"
bound there

to what's further in.
The tenancies of Traherne-
like creatures

are composed
almost entirely of such melodies
and could dissolve at any moment.

To defend against this they bare
their teeth at the savage ether
and watch from a distance

as others drag down lithe deer
and small dogs. They track
any ill-hidden cache—

raiding it
as soon as fresh snow falls
creating a shadowy newness.

In Confidence

We found a body face down in the swells,
floating and dragging in time—
rust-red organisms cleaved to it.

It was a silent climate.
Floor or ceiling, it was dense and luxe.
Breathing. Just breathing.

We sent it to a lab
that could make electrons spin
then slow then counter-spin

to reveal a forest in the saltiest fluid.
It emitted a continuous low-pitch drizzle of concern
such as adults emit as they adjust

their not-yet's and nocturnal whispers.
All we had was the starched, psychic instruments
of our good clothes.

What else could we have done
with these near-human amplitudes
that pulsed the bay?

There was an echo in our voice,
and water, and earth. And you
at the mouth, strange species.

The sea was animal, vegetable, and mineral.
It seized
and held us fast where the eyes went.

Awe Applied by Degree

The state of wonder has agents
authorized to hold us fast
by the pulp in our reason.

It's bought up our debt
and exhaled itself in the body's vault,
made inquiries into our fleshy

tabernacles and offices. It likes to look
while we sit on the cot,
the floor, the toilet. It repeats,

The way of science always bleeds
into violence. The state of wonder
is prepossessed with a sadness

as infinitely divisible as the continent
it's driven across,
pressed in a low-lying front.

What else could it need?
Our doubt is born in full bloom,
fully sentient, by which

I mean quivering
from snout to anus, exposing itself
to the wind on purpose.

2. Low Magic

I felt my life with both my hands
To see if it was there—
I held my spirit to the Glass,
To prove it possibler—

—Emily Dickinson

(　　)

The Bishop of Bamberg

This is how he lived, with messianic faith
in his uniqueness. Each parishioner he touched,
he became. This was mostly to the good. Gracious
and stiff with his hand on the burgomaster's cloak.
Pedantic and disappointed when slipping the Body of Christ
onto a righteous tongue. But then a whoreson dog
gave him carbuncles and a flaming ass, and the hog
he swallowed left him feeling botched and flayed.
He thought fit to drink some medicine and vomit up
his disease, then had it purged out from below. Submitted
to burning, then cutting. This is how he lived, the Bishop
of Bamberg, who sent his flock to wait in line at Lourdes
while he directed himself to the profane waters
of Karlsbad, then Kissingen. He thought he was curing the pig,
the pig was curing him. The Bishop knew full well
that it is not matter that defines life. Process,
such as energy flow, does. An entire man, he felt
all his needs by turns—touching each creature in his ken,
its needs were his—and took nothing as an equivalent
for life but the fullness of living itself. He was
utterly carefree in his efforts to elude death, choosing
the diameter and density of the metal rod

for his own hand, saw it attached to comb-like spikes.
Now, turn the handle that spins the glass cylinder
against a silk swatch to make a charge. It makes
a charge. He smokes. He lives.

O Procurador

The Franciscan friars of the cloister of St. Anthony
in the province of Piedade no Maranhão, Brazil,
were besieged by termites who descended in a cloud
upon their food, their furniture, even the earthen walls.

The decision to prosecute was swift and total,
made by attorneys intent on a justice
that would move the spirit as it moved the bodies.
But the soul appointed to the vermin promised

a vigorous defense—for the white ants' industry
was far superior to that of their prosecutors, and, too,
they held the right of prior possession, having
occupied the land untold eons before the Church.

It was an argument larded with precedent
and led in all grace and justice to a decision
the termites themselves had to accept.
At a time and place the judge in the name

of Lord God pronounced, they marched in columns
to a reservation—newly sited, tabulated, discrete.
What was once impossible to divide
had been fully accounted for until such time

as fire and flood reclaim.

The Burgomaster of Ansbach

In 1685 the burgomaster of Ansbach
was reincarnated as a werewolf.
He preyed upon the herds, savaged

children and drove blunt-headed men
to gnashing despair.
There came a day when the beast

was tracked and killed.
The inconsolable mob
stretched over the creature's carcass

a skintight suit
made of flesh-colored cere-cloth,
adorned him in a chestnut brown wig

and long whitish beard.
They hacked off his snout and slipped
a mask over his skull

freshly painted with the burgomaster's
own dire features.
The counterfeit was hanged

by order of the court about the neck
until twice dead. In the councils
that followed, people drank only spirits

that had been thoroughly distilled.
It was—and remains—a technology
for separating the inseparable.

One Possible Universe

Leibniz asked, why did the universe start when it did and not ten minutes later?

The knife-fish *Gymnarchus* swims backwards without bumping into anything,

but when you comb your hair near its tank, the electrical discharge sends the creature into a frenzy of desire and confusion.

Dystiscus, the diving beetle, hides a single bubble of air under its wing as it descends to the river bottom clutching its companion.

A wizard strolls among vegetables in a time of fear and greed and makes the roofers laugh hideously until the cabbage worms come and cover them under.

I have read in books that a man's erotic duty is a matter of public necessity;

that a fish, a donkey, the nimble-minded hoodie crow all have sufficient songs and reasons and sexes.

And still we find ourselves in this never-ending city.

And still our conflicts give rise to heat and excess of possibility.

Balaam in Winter

And so it is with me as it was with Balaam, the confused prophet who blessed
when he had come to curse.
—Goethe

Among stinkbugs under the snowpack, among Indiana bats, Norwegian
rats, and woodchucks big as bouncers, among hospice managers shivering
in goose-down and cubicle dwellers agitating to the square inch, among
the ragged, the crooked, the strung out and the shining, among Spanish
clementines aglow in balsa crates and pear buds dense under bare
branches, daffodil bulbs packed in plastic and stacked out on the street,
among baked brick buildings that sculpt the air in great shoves and cold
shoulders, first I sat quietly; then I squeaked like a mouse in distress. All
my predators and consumables alike were occupied in separate torpor. I
sat by a hole in the ground and I waited—for the curse to come, for my
hunger, for fear, for someone to bring me flowers for my bed, for rain, for
locusts thick enough to eat, for a talking donkey to tell me what to do, for
one frank death or a vision of what comes next.

Schütze

The poet was drawn to the shapely ears
of his friend Schütze, a Frankfurt native
Maestro asked to sit
perfectly still one Italian evening.

But Schütze was seized by an uncontrollable
fit of the giggles thanks to the circum-
locutions of Hoffrat Reiffenstein,
a pompous ass who was saying something

about art and imitation and how
one proceeds to greatness
holding an endless train of thought
by its naked edge.

Percival Lowell tried to interject
that Consciousness is just nerve glow,
but got nowhere.
He wanted his thread of reasoning

to be a "bee line" a solitary worker makes
when it knows exactly what reward
awaits and how many patriots
of its colony have made it

there and back again. But his words
only partially explained the giggles,
and could not touch the roundabout
thinking that led to them

nor explain how badly they shook
the boy's body
until there was nothing left but the wayward
undulations of the flesh.

Our Barbarian Fathers

It is a difficult and melancholy business
separating old ideas from the new,
drawing out flavors of caramel, oak,
and purest ethanol from appellation
cognac, beaker by beaker in San Francisco.

Our barbarian fathers, lords of black powder,
left in us a moneyed sense of taste
we employ to destroy ourselves.
You can tell in each sip how America's
coke has oak in it and caramel, too.

Burn it until it's char then smear the char
on the walls in depictions both beautiful and true.
Cities were built on this design: cluster, scorch,
and raise. I come from both those
who crossed the short sea to slaughter

and those they slaughtered. I come
from graptolites living together in horny sheaths.
"O Universe! what thou wishest I wish,"
said Marcus Aurelius. Or, as they say
in the Capitol, "If it's happening, be *for* it."

Consciousness is a new state of nature
to which our bodies are ill-adapted,
slave to the greatest fawning and self-tyranny,
full of fear, overflowing with convulsions and pains,
resembling the disposition of our own frantic city.

Roman law proclaimed, Sons and daughters
should suffer their parents' punishment
since they'll soon enough be guilty
of the same crime themselves.

( )

In a World of Ruins

there was something to be grateful for.
My brother's bed too dark to see,
unmoored somewhere off in the night

I couldn't bear. My parents' starlit tree
flowering pink and white
with buds I'd spent all day splitting

and chewing and spitting out into a paste
cupped in my hand. My father's car
zipping open the gravel drive with the top down,

a fountain of dust billowing behind us.
All this exists only in my head. The people
I was there with still live as I do, but don't

recall a thing. How did all our pasts
get so different? The longer
I live the less I feel like myself.

Medical literature suggests I'm lucky
to have chosen 1967 for a birth year,
as if those four numbers whirred up

on a slot machine, granting me treatment
denied others. One infant's illness
is another's opportunity. So what

animal then did my holding on
push off the shelf? Maybe it was myself
I replaced since being has a re-

cursive quality. Everywhere I walk,
the ground trembles
as when a fox pounds snow for a mouse.

Once upon a once upon a—
nothing. Then something. Something.
Nothing. This city is made entirely of snow.

The Brothers

Thank god everything we saw today has been sufficiently described already.

How inner hairs convert sound waves into electrical impulses.

How a white-faced hornet stirs dead wood she's scraped together with her spit into a papier-mâché palace for her daughters.

How Bartholomew Chassenée made his reputation at the bar as counsel for a mischief of rats.

How Syrian women rubbed amber jewelry up against wool to make a static field.

How I pried off the cedar walls my brother built, to steal his glass and coins.

How the neighbor boy smashed my wrist, then pledged fealty to me for the error.

How I broke the rule of No Knives so I could carve my name into the magnolia branch outside my mother's window.

How Dr. Barnes left us to the severed heads our brothers chose, hyena and gazelle to watch over our beds.

How our father consorted with kings and oilmen, spies and thieves.

How his business gave shape to our days with its comings and goings.

And the day his return was met with packed bags that contained "everything he needs"?

I was warned by our mother, weren't you? I was told. It was just.

We were not ourselves secured in the bags, of course, being children not rats squirming warm in the undercarriage. He did not ask us to be.

Some cell always gets between the stimulus and the nerves that lead to the brain.

What separates, connects. A sterner, more wonderful joy.

Patrimony

A dad walks into a bar and feels his wit melt a little bit, sag at the edges like his tits.

A dad resembles a landscape where nature acts in the falling away and collapsing together of unlike parts. He walks into a bar

and tries to find a game, the dribble penetration that leads to an outside shot, the domination of the paint that means crashing the boards.

A dad feels consciousness dissolve out of his matter through coarsened pores, a heightened periodicity in the folds of his skin that implies time

is quickening even as his body slows and this moment now grows broader, stretchier, shows layers underneath and overhead he hadn't noticed before.

A dad has children but they seem to be elsewhere. Do they even exist? If they don't then he's no dad.

There's a game on the big screen filled with other people's sons. If his own exist but don't know him, then he's still a dad in theory but not in practice.

If he could just do that thing with money he doesn't understand, it would all add up to continuance, procedure, a long line. Here at the bar he walks into, at the bar he walks up to. If he could just complete one action. How can the floor be so sticky and slippery at the same time?

This whole existence as a dad is a *hysteron proteron*, an agitation to shoot before the ball itself has arrived.

It can be rectified by putting this dad in the position of a son who is lost and enters the bar looking for someone to claim him.

Ipso facto, post facto. Let's try this again.

Sensible & True

Mornings the mist is a breathing thing
when she greets me, all
Viking smile and gardener's hands
battered blue and gold.

Does it matter she died half a year ago
or that even dead she's kept
her talent for pissing me off with that look
that says is this what I

should really be doing with the day?
The consequences of wasted time
are only more of an open question now
with her half-here, half-vanished

in the half-light of dawn.
Tis here Tis here Tis gone.
How in all this do I make or find
an equilibrium to call my own?

There are at least as many states of rest
as there are human enterprises.
It's time to choose words again,
to make some way—even if it's just

a path toward the exit.

        One friend traded his music for gold,

    another his body

for the velvety slosh of grandeur.

They did so well! But to them,

        each choice still looks as much like folly

    as the one I made to give

and give and give to air,

believing as I did that air was all there was.

        When did *choose-your-own-adventure*

    become *become-your-own-end?*

My sister, who could offer some insight into this,

stays zip-lipped at the foot of the bed

        in a way that's both comforting

    and unsettling. I think maybe

she's not sure she's really here.

We each have a belief that's path-dependent.

        Mine says she exists;

    hers, she doesn't. Listen. Our present

circumstances depend not just

on where we are but how we got here.

The departments of housing, sex, sleep, etc.

Now, eleven flights up,

here I am, talking to you,

and a bee appears in the window box.

A miracle! That's what I mean.

Take what you need brother,

pass it along.

The Last Resort

The town was built as an escape from towns. The sea grasped with iron piers. The walls and walkways scrubbed and scoured and set with pebbles you could fit into your mouth. There was just enough room for a body to be stretched out upon the sand by the litter bearers. Just enough airspace to hear the sacred geese give warning that our enemies were near, crouched on the horizon. Nature loves to hide. Yes, and nature loves to find itself out by means of surprise. Was that a conversation of barely audible *tsees* in the spruce thicket? No doubt about it, and they were coming closer; a kinglet never holds still for more than a second. *Corvus corax* clustered in pairs. *Vulpes vulpes* colluded in dens. We were not in the thickety wood and that was by choice. Today I shall write a few words and let one letter chase another, and then I will send you, sisters and brothers, scrambling after them beyond the walls.

( )

Coming Through

My first two years in this foreign land
were taken up largely with experiments
in thought-transference and those

largely with a pair of clergyman's daughters
who seemed to possess the power of guessing secret
occupations across vast, velvety plains of matter.

Maybe it was just physics, or physiological psychology,
both of which are supposed to bar the way to old faith
only to create fresh paths that lead straight back to it.

We lie in the lap of immense intelligence,
my faithful counselor wrote to me, bending my mind
slow as cabbage around the weight of his argument

as planets are bent in orbit and bend,
which makes us both receivers of its truth
and agents of its activity.

Maybe there are many minds behind the scenes, not one.
Maybe I'm one of them, struggling in this remote
and distant room before a blindingly bright window

that looks out on a wall of blindingly bright windows
and you, who are what I want, grow infinite to me,
expanding as quickly as you recede.

American Cockroach

Your alien hairs extend in twin
prongs from your forehead, sway
in articulations

Fred Astaire's arms once assumed,
slowing, steering time.
Snared glint of a thing,

you wave and I wave back.
Summerhot countertop
varnish buckles and sucks

at my hands. I can hardly see
for the sweat that grows
a second skin on my eyeballs.

You tickle the baseboard, festooned
in shadow, ribboned
in mystery, as ridiculously animate

and alive as a thumb.
I'm struck dumb
by your brisk and tender regard—

feed it, cracking
the lid on these sour grounds,
rotted petals,

frank curds and jolly ranchers
all clumped together. These are your
explicit necessities

for eating, shitting, and making eggs.
It's not an offering I give you,
but it's good you gather what you need

from the resin of our shared afternoon.
Do you extend your limbs a touch
toward guilt, or innocence?

The Turtle

I was without imagination because I was without experience.
—Bernd Heinrich

What's death to a turtle
that winters through
with almost no heart activity,

whose legs retract to the touch
for hours after its head
has been clapped off by an ax?

The fact of itself is a kind of thought,
or even, electrically,
a feeling, a fiction of its own continuance.

The turtle has dreams and madness
as I do—ephemeral
guardians of the need for a piece

of chipmunk or hamburger
from a scientist's green glove.
The season makes everything

frivolous but food.

A good prod gets a snap back.
What kind of thought is that

but proximity, velocity,
probability.
It's the only reality

the turtle and I have.
Each new mind creates its own
companionable room

to live in, buried under
river ice or packed in frozen
aquarium dirt. Do you hear

how the struck-white harbor
east of here is beginning
to crackle and boom? Head for it.

Foxed

Marshal us, rye-stained snout and glassine teeth.

Electric engine, as Klimt would have it.

Sun god, let us dine on sturgeon.

Pressure is the force of lift,

a natural bounce antipodal

to the run of snow.

Versailles would do, none too swift

to be swallowed like a tongue by the *Galerie des Glaces*.

One clot, punctured.

Tiny piston,

frail instrument, your hie skirt slackens

and makes for the far trees—

a reddish, uncertain dark.

The Warblers Are Come

The warblers are come
and it's a different world.
Bare branches swollen,

eleven stories below.
A sharp gust snares the dew
and carries it up

through the window.
I lift my hand to wet my lips.
It's quiet enough to listen to.

Garbage bags whistle
and pop like fireworks in the truck's ass.
South of here, the song goes on

in the rickhouse. They're
binding up slow growth timber
tight, since closer rings

make higher
levels of tannin and hemicellulose
available to the spirit.

So, we like to drink wood.
It tastes good,
noble even, even as the chemicals

tune human blood to the desire
to sink your head
neck-deep in a barrel.

*

Once upon a time in a northern April,
I found a bevy of young flying squirrels
with still-closed eyes

and took one home
in my shirt pocket to nurse and raise
as my own. The geranium sprig

in the dish on my windowsill
looked like the most fragile thing
in the room, a thing at the end

of its own good time.
Was it the fresh-looking water

or the flower
or the squirrel's own flickering mind
that begged
the creature sip until it retched and fell

stone dead on the carpet?

*

There was a thought-god who said,
"Every outward good
becomes mere weariness to the flesh."

A dull, continuous ache abides in the head,
begs you to move.
No, captor, my captor, *commands* you

cross the running stream
you dare not cross—a bird afloat
with a foamy neck, pressed by the wind

to swallow what it cuts through.

( )

Mysterious Pulse

"Oh mysterious pulse!"   César Vallejo
said as he pointed   to his wrist.
It throbbed,   shackled as it was,
exquisite and corrupt.   He wanted out.
He wanted in.   Light and shadow
coupling. He pointed   not to the metal
but to the flesh   within the metal
that beat in time   with his heart
and his lungs   and his liver,
as it beats now   in mine, an echo
of what we know   in what we don't.

Slow Gold

March opens to a distant hook,
sound-balloon
burst from a ruffled goose
or trial saxophone. Any flagrant
yellow in the vein
of forsythia is a partial start.
All devices on sleep buzz
in place like bugs in high summer.
They're all turned on. Turn me
one notch down, please,
my head's full of furze.
Spring birds
make a morning note
by note. Sharp and sweet,
the same sound carbonation bubbles make
out from under a loose cap.
Or the noise machine we calibrate
to Bardo panic. It doesn't help us
snooze, just masks the trucks.
Another consciousness held too fast to.
The radiators have something else to lose,
loose steam transported

in the pipes sezz *esses zizzes*
zzz's you wake up to. One warm day
and all the flowers will pop.

After Lighght

Look, I've already ruined it
or it's ruined me.
The dawn I see by doesn't need me

like I need it
and any extra letters it brings.
What we call mountains

is a deep violet strip
narrowly rising and falling over the green.
You might call them clouds

and be right
or hand me something crisp
call it money or flowers

and set it alight.

Notes

"Did I grow or did I stay? Did I vanish or decay?" I'm nearly certain
Thomas Traherne wrote this, but cannot find the actual citation.

"Homage to the EEG": cf. *Homenaje a la epilepsia* by Jaime Saenz

"The Body and the Bed": "A tongue of light, a fit of flame" —Coleridge; "I
could not wish to be rid of it"—Teresa of Avila

"Interictal": "Disturbance of the functions of the animal economy of the
soul" is the fourth definition of the noun form of "Disorder" listed in
Webster's 1913 ed.

"Surgeon": "Open, boisterous sea" Roman (Julius Caesar's?) description of
the English Channel

"Homage to the Electrodes Fixed to Your Scalp": Clare of Assisi said the bit
at the end, or John Clare implied it.

"Peak Phosphorous": "No other remedy . . . but absolute departure."
—Milton

"Awe Applied by Degree":"Fleshy: Human. [Obs.] Fleshy tabernacle. —
Milton" Webster's 1913 ed.

"I felt my life with both my hands..." is by Emily Dickinson

"In a World of Ruins": The first sentence is from Goethe's *Italian Journey,* in
which G. goes on to say "The immensity of the place has a quieting effect."

"Sensible and True": Horatio says of Old Hamlet's ghost: "I might not this
believe / Without the sensible and true avouch / Of mine own eyes."

"The Bishop of Bamberg" et al.: "Although all men insisted on being spoken
to by the universe in some way, few insisted on being spoken to in the same
way." —Wm. James

"The Bishop," "O Procurador," "The Burgomaster," and the wizard in "One

Possible Universe" are indebted to *The Criminal Prosecution and Punishment of Animals* by Edward Payson Evans (especially "The Burgomaster") and *The Spark of Life* by Frances Ashcroft (especially "The Bishop").

"Our Barbarian Fathers" is indebted to *Proof: The Science of Booze* by Adam Rogers.

"Schütze" is after Goethe's *Italian Journey* (wherein we meet Schütze and Riffenstein). Percival Lowell's conjecture is related in William James' *The Varieties of Religious Experience*.

"Coming Through" is indebted to Wm. James' *Varieties...*

"The Turtle and the Warblers" are indebted to Bernd Heinrich's *Winter World*.

"Slow Gold" is for Lygia Pape, whose *Divisor* drew me out across the park to see it

"After Lighght" is after Aram Saroyan's "lighght."

Acknowledgments

Thanks to those whose own writing and care with these poems made this a better book, especially Michael Morse and Geoffrey Nutter—and Miranda, of course, whose attentive genius sparked and shaped and fueled and spirited everything here from the first words to the last.

Thanks to the editors and readers of the following journals and newsletters in which some of the book's poems have appeared:

Academy of American Poets Poem-a-Day Newsletter, *Bennington Review*, *Black Clock*, *Boston Review*, *The Colorado Review*, *The Literary Review*, *Ladowich*, and *Oversound*.

And to the anthology *Infiltration: An Anthology of Innovative Poetry from the Hudson River Valley* (Station Hill of Barrytown, 2016) in which "Stout Cortez" appeared (as "Suddenly, the Guards Return to the Priest Called 'Stout Cortez'").

"Death Is Death" won the Emily Dickinson Award from the Poetry Society of America. Thanks to judge Dan Beachy-Quick and the good people at the PSA.

Tom Thompson is also the author of *Live Feed* and *The Pitch*. He lives in New York City with his wife, Miranda Field, and their two sons.

Publication of this book was made possible by grants and donations. We are also grateful to those individuals who participated in our 2017 Build a Book Program. They are:

Anonymous (6), Evan Archer, Sally Ball, Vincent Bell, Jan Bender-Zanoni, Zeke Berman, Kristina Bicher, Laurel Blossom, Carol Blum, Betsy Bonner, Mary Brancaccio, Lee Briccetti, Deirdre Brill, Anthony Cappo, Carla & Steven Carlson, Caroline Carlson, Stephanie Chang, Tina Chang, Liza Charlesworth, Paula Colangelo, Maxwell Dana, Machi Davis, Marjorie Deninger, Emily Flitter, Lukas Fauset, Monica Ferrell, Jennifer Franklin, Helen Fremont & Donna Thagard, Robert Fuentes & Martha Webster, Chuck Gillett, Dorothy Goldman, Dr. Lauri Grossman, Naomi Guttman & Jonathan Mead, Steven Haas, Mary & John Heilner, Hermann Hesse, Deming Holleran, Nathaniel Hutner, Janet Jackson, Christopher Kempf, David Lee, Jen Levitt, Howard Levy, Owen Lewis, Paul Lisicky, Sara London & Dean Albarelli, David Long, Katie Longofono, Cynthia Lowen, Ralph & Mary Ann Lowen, Donna Masini, Louise Mathias, Catherine McArthur, Nathan McClain, Victoria McCoy, Gregory McDonald, Britt Melewski, Kamilah Moon, Carolyn Murdoch, Rebecca & Daniel Okrent, Tracey Orick, Zachary Pace, Gregory Pardlo, Allyson Paty, Veronica Patterson, Marcia & Chris Pelletiere, Maya Pindyck, Taylor Pitts, Eileen Pollack, Barbara Preminger, Kevin Prufer, Vinode Ramgopal, Martha Rhodes, Peter & Jill Schireson, Roni & Richard Schotter, Andrew Seligsohn, Soraya Shalforoosh, Peggy Shinner, James Snyder & Krista Fragos, Alice St. Claire-Long, Megan Staffel, Robin Taylor, Marjorie & Lew Tesser, Boris Thomas, Judith Thurman, Susan Walton, Calvin Wei, Abby Wender, Bill Wenthe, Allison Benis White, Elizabeth Whittlesey, Hao Wu, Monica Youn, and Leah Zander.